Dr. D. K. Olukoya

The Power of Aggressive

PRAYER
WARRIORS

The Power of Aggressive Prayer Warriors

DR. D. K. OLUKOYA

(2) Dr. D. K. OLUKOYA

THE POWER OF AGGRESSIVE PRAYER WARRIORS

© 2009 DR. D. K. OLUKOYA

ISBN **978-0692374993**

November 2009

Published by:

Mountain of Fire and Miracles Ministries Press

13, Olasimbo Street, Onike, Yaba, Lagos.

All Scripture quotation is from the King James Version of the Bible

All rights reserved.

We prohibit reproduction in whole or part without written permission.

TABLE OF CONTENTS

1. THE POWER OF AGGRESSIVE PRAYER WARRIORS 4
2. MILITANCY IN PRAYERS 13
3. POWER OVER THE ENEMY 23
4. VICTORY OVER SATANIC MESSENGERS 34
5. THE SATANIC VESSEL 35
6. PRAYER POINTS 42

(4) Dr. D. K. OLUKOYA

CHAPTER ONE

THE POWER OF AGGRESSIVE PRAYER WARRIORS

THE POWER OF AGGRESSIVE PRAYER WARRIORS (5)

"Now Amalek came and fought with Israel in Rephidim and Moses said to Joshua, Choose us some men and go out and fight with Amalek. Tomorrow I will stand on top of the hill with the rod of God in my hand. So Joshua did as Moses said to him and fought with Amalek. And Moses, Aaron and Hur went up to the top of the hill. And so it was, when Moses held up his hand, that Israel prevailed, and when he let down his hand, Amalek prevailed. But Moses hands became heavy, so they took a stone and put it under him, and he sat thereon; And Aaron and Hur stayed up his hands, the one on the one side and the other on the other side, and his hands were steady until the going down of the sun. So Joshua discomfitted Amalek and his people with the edge of the sword. Then the Lord said to Moses, write this for a memorial in the book and recount it in the hearing of Joshua that I will blot out the remembrance of Amalek from under heaven. And Moses built an altar and called its name; JEHOVAH NISSI, (meaning, THE LORD IS MY BANNER). For he said, because the Lord has sworn, the Lord will have war with Amalek from generation to generation." Exodus 17:8-16.

There was a battle between the Amalekites and the Israelites. The physical battle was going on down the hill, but Moses knew that before you could get anything to work in the physical it would first of all have to work in the spiritual. So, he fought spiritually. As he prayed, the battle came in favour of the Israelites, but anytime his hands were weak, the Amalekites prevailed against the Israelites.

THE FLOW

Many people do not really know much about prayer before they practise praying. But the truth is that God's power can only flow to people who pray and pray aright. The Bible says, "The Lord is a man of war and the LORD is His name." So, our Commander-in-chief is a warrior and a fighter. Prayer is an important part of that war.

If we look at this story again we can see that Moses prayed while Joshua fought and he found out that he must keep his hands stretched out to heaven in prayer, if he must open the door for God's supernatural intervention. He discovered that God's prevailing power was released through prayer and that this power was released into the lives of those who pray. It would be hard for God to release His power into your life if you do not take praying as a serious business. Prayerless people cut themselves off from God's prevailing power. Prayerless people are overwhelmed, over run, beaten down, pushed around and defeated by the enemy.

THE ANGEL

Immediately Moses could make the connection between prayer and God's power, his prayers began to yield results at the battle. Jesus said, "Men ought always to pray, and not faint. He did not say, "Men ought always to sing," or "men ought always to preach."

(8) Dr. D. K. OLUKOYA

There is nothing too great, too hard or too difficult that prayer cannot do. It has obtained things that seemed to be out of reach. It has won victories over fire, water and death. It was prayer that parted the Red sea. "So shall your Red sea part today, in Jesus' name." Prayer brought water out of the rock and bread from heaven. What does that mean? It means that your impossible situations can become possible through prayers.

A long time ago, at one of our business meetings, I shared the testimony of a man who was a prayer warrior. He would come to the church and pray his heart out, but he was poor and people were laughing at him. When contributions were to be made to buy certain things, this prayer warrior would not be able to make any. Many times he actually suffered open ridicule from some brethren. So, at a point he got discouraged and sat at home. The people did not know that it was the prayer of that man that God respected most. Immediately he walked out on the church problems started.

The city council brought a letter that the church should be moved because a road was to be constructed there. They called a prayer meeting quickly and started praying to God that the council would change its mind. During the prayer meeting, there was a word of prophecy: "You have chased the angel out of this place. You better go and look for him."

Eventually, somebody was sent to the poor man's house to beg him to come back to the church. When he came back and they prayed together, to the glory of God, another letter came from the council stating that there was a mistake by one of their engineers, that the road would not pass through the church. This was a clear demonstration of the power of prayer.

This man kept coming and God was always saying to him, "I am going to make you a millionaire without you raising a finger." He did not understand. But one day, as he finished praying the Lord said, "Go to the beach now." As a good prayer warrior, he obeyed the Lord and went, praying on the way. When he got to the beach, he saw a corked bottle floating on the water. Eventually, the wave brought the bottle ashore. He ran, picked and opened it and saw that there was a piece of paper that looked like a cheque leaf inside. He forced the paper out, opened and read it.

THE MIRACLE

The paper was a will by one very rich man somewhere in who never married and had no children or relatives when he died. He left this will in which he instructed that half of his wealth should be given to his dog and the other half to anybody that would find the will in the bottle. That was what this man found! So, the man who could not afford to come to church by bus, became a millionaire.

Indeed, prayer can turn a person's situation around. Prayer made the sun to stand still. This means that the enemy will not be able to introduce darkness that will hinder your breakthrough and the sun shall stand still until victory is yours. Prayer brings fire from the sky and so shall help come to you from above too, in

Jesus' name. Prayer turned the counsel of Ahitophel into foolishness. So shall every evil counsel against you be turned to foolishness, in Jesus' name. And I know that all my Ahitophel shall receive confusion, in Jesus' name.

THE POWER OF PRAYER

It was prayer that overthrew the army of Senacherib when it encamped against the children of God. Because of prayer, the Lord sent just one angel that destroyed 185,000 soldiers. So shall all the enemies encamped against you be put to shame, in Jesus' name.

You may wonder: can a person have up to 185,000 enemies? Oh yes. There was one man in the Bible, who had 6,000 demons living inside him and he was still moving about. Some black people have more than that and they are still drinking beer in the streets. Sometimes you wonder how someone can drink a whole carton of beer. He is not the one drinking it. A white man friend of mine used to say, "The child of many prayers can never perish."

A lot of people wonder why they pray but still have attacks. The Bible says, "Pray without ceasing." It means that as you continue to pray, something good must happen. But if you cease, something bad will happen, because we have an enemy who never ceases to attack, who does not sleep. Some people take sleeping pills when they cannot get enough sleep. But the enemies of the souls of men do not sleep at all, they are ceaseless devourers.

When God told Moses that He wanted to destroy the people of Israel because of their stubbornness and make of him a great new nation, he said no and began to appeal to God not to destroy them. His prayer held God's hand. As long as Abraham was asking for mercy on behalf of Sodom and Gomorrah, the Lord was granting it and did not cease until Abraham stopped. May be if he had gone further and said, "Supposing you find one," Sodom and Gomorrah would have been saved. But he stopped at asking for 10 and the Lord stopped at 10 too.

CHAPTER TWO
MILITANCY IN PRAYERS

(14) Dr. D. K. OLUKOYA

As God's children, beloved, we are supposed to do all our things militantly. We read the Bible militantly, speak militantly, evangelise militantly and pray militantly, because God is not a civilian, but a soldier.

"Now I saw heaven open, and behold, a white horse. And he that sat upon him was called faithful and true, and in righteousness He doth judge and make a war. His eyes were as a flame of fire, and on His head were many crowns, and he had a name written, that no man knew but he himself. And he was clothed with a robe dipped in blood: and his name is called the word of God. And the armies which were in heaven, followed him upon white horses. Clothed in fine linen, white and clean. And out of His mouth goeth a sharp sword, that with it He should smite the nations: and he shall rule them with a rod of iron: and he treadeth the winepress of the fierceness and wrath of Almighty God. And he hath on His vesture and on His thigh a name written King of kings and Lord of Lords." Revelation 19:11-14.

THE POWER OF AGGRESSIVE PRAYER WARRIORS (15)

The Lord himself is a man of war. So, when you pray, you are employing a very powerful military strategy. The most useful soldiers in the army of the Lord are the prayer warriors. Satan has raised up a great antagonism against prayer and launches his violent attacks on any ministry of prayer. He tries to ensure that people do not pray. He wants to ensure that nobody prays and if he fails in doing that, he makes sure that the prayer is weak. If he fails in that too, he manipulates the person to pray civilian prayers, that is, useless prayers, prayers that will go up and bring down nothing.

MILITANT PRAYERS

Militant prayer must have power and fire in it. It must get the supernatural power of God to work in overcoming problems and unprofitable situations. When you pray militantly, you rise from your knees refreshed. When you pray and rise up weak and wary, know that you have prayed the civilian way. Militant prayer is a powerful weapon. It has the capacity to issue embarrassing surprises on the enemies, because they can never know what you are going to say next or your direction. This is part of the reason the devil fears prayer, especially by somebody who prays in the Holy Ghost. Militant prayer can turn the table in favour of the minority.

Peter was put in prison with very tight security and there was no way he could get out. Why did they take that kind of precaution on Peter? They did because they had thrown some apostles into jail before and an angel came, opened the door and said, "All of you walk out, go back to the market, where they caught you and start preaching there again." So, 16 soldiers were attached to Peter and he was tied with two chains.

But something happened. His miracle did not come late. The doors opened, the chains broke, the soldiers did not know and Peter walked out. The doors opened for Peter on their own accord without anybody touching them. It will be wise, beloved, that you too pray like this: "Let the doors of breakthrough open for me by their own accord, in the name of Jesus."

CHARACTERISTICS OF MILITANT PRAYERS

1. Militant prayer must be anointed and not one taken from a 17th century book that has no relevance to your life now. It must be done in a divine presence. Jesus prayed at a particular place and the Bible says that His countenance changed. When you pray without the anointing, you chase away the presence of God.

2. It is prayer filled with determination. There is nothing many of us can achieve in the school of holiness if we cannot stay long alone with God in persistent prayer. The forces wanting to pull people down are so many and the Bible laments: "How are the mighty fallen and the weapons of war perish." You just have to pray with more determination and persistence like Jacob.

3. It must be specific and intensive, not just anything. There are many promises for the believer in the Bible. So you must be specific when you pray. When blind Bartimaeus screamed, Jesus asked him,

"What do you want me to do for you?" So, be specific. It is an insult for a man to be asking God for things that are of no value. So, in your prayer, call a spade a spade.

4. It must be according to God's will.

5. It must not be cold. It must have life. We must not offer dead prayers through laziness. Laziness in prayer will cause trouble for you.

6. It must be said with violent faith, believing God for a breakthrough.

7. It must be bold. In other words, it must have holy boldness.

As a military strategy, prayer must be said with militant aggression, military tactics and with a sense of purpose. We must remember that the battle is the

Lord's and that victory has been given to us. We are only battle axes in the hand of the mighty God of war. If we yield ourselves as effectual instrument of prayer in our God's hands, we are sure to win any enemy that confronts us, in Jesus' name.

PRAYER POINTS

1. Every stronghold of wickedness fashioned against me, let the fire of God burn you to ashes, in the name of Jesus.

2. Every ritual and sacrifice working against me, be neutralised, in the name of Jesus.

3. Every evil bird delegated against me, fall down to the ground and die, in the name of Jesus.

4. You drinkers of blood, my family and I are not your candidates, in the name of Jesus.

5. I refuse to dwell in the building constructed for me by my enemies, in the name of Jesus.

6. Let the blessings, presence, domination and authority of God be experienced in every

department of my life, in the name of Jesus.

7. I destroy every satanic establishment against my life, in the name of Jesus.

8. I break every satanic co-operation against my life, in the name of Jesus.

9. I command confusion and disagreement upon my hardened enemies, in the name of Jesus.

10. I break every covenant formed by my enemies against me, in the name of Jesus.

11. I paralyse every spirit of wastage, I shall not borrow, in the name of Jesus.

12. I paralyse every evil hand pointing at my blessing, in the name of Jesus.

13. I withdraw every satanic instruction targeted at me, in the name of Jesus.

14. Enough is enough of hidden and open infirmity, in the name of Jesus.

15. Every evil river, dry up. And every evil shrine working against me, be roasted, in the name of Jesus

16. I crush every battle of the enemy, in the name of Jesus.

17. I refuse to be subdued by the forces of wickedness, in the name of Jesus.

18. I refuse to be fed with the bread of sorrow, in the name of Jesus.

19. I nullify every night arrow fired against me, in the name of Jesus.

20. I issue death sentence on all my Goliaths, in the name of Jesus.

21. My miracle will not die, in the name of Jesus.

22. My testimony will not vanish, in the name of Jesus.

23. My dream will not become a nightmare, in the name of Jesus.

24. Devil, you are a liar, you cannot capture my destiny, in the name of Jesus.

25. I refuse to waste my divine opportunity, in the name of Jesus.

26. Every authority challenging the move of God in my life, be paralysed, in the name of Jesus.

27. I break every agreement made between my parents and satan on my behalf, in the name of Jesus.

CHAPTER THREE
POWER OVER THE ENEMY

Do you know that as a child of God, you have the power to harass the enemy instead of the enemy harassing you? This is because Jesus overcame satan and has given you power over the enemy. Let us consider some examples in the Bible where Jesus harassed the enemy. In Mark 5, we read about the demon-possessed man who came to Jesus.

"And cried with a loud voice, and said, what have I to do with thee, Jesus, thou Son of the most high God? I adjure thee by God, that thou torment me not." Mark 5:7.

THE ENEMY'S FEAR

That spirit was begging not to be tormented, meaning that he could be tormented. In Luke 8:30-31 also, we see some spirits begging our Lord Jesus.

"And Jesus asked him, saying, what is thy name? And he said, Legion; because many devils were entered into him. And they besought him that he would not command them to go out into the deep."

So, there is a place the spirits are afraid to go. They begged Jesus, "Please, do anything you want to do to us but do not send us to that place."

"Thou believest that there is one God, thou doest well, the devils also believe, and tremble." James 2:19.

The Bible teaches that all these powers harassing us can be harassed as well. It tells us that there are places they would prefer you do not send them. The Scriptures also teach us that we can make demons to tremble.

ABNORMAL!

The devil is very wicked. He has really dealt with humanity. One man came to me and said, "Pastor, I have a problem." I said, "What is the problem?" He said, "You see, I slept with my sister." I said, "Are both of you of the same parents?" He said, "Yes." I told him that it was no problem, that God would forgive him. He said, "That is not all, my father slept with her too." I said, "Ha! That is serious." As a man of God, how would you react to that? You could say these people are bad; a terrible father and a terrible son. But, is that the answer? No. There is a spirit that pushed them to do evil.

There are many things people cover up and are unable to talk about because most people would not understand them. They just cover them up and many of them are Christians. They love God, sing praise worship and do all kinds of things. It is a rape of humanity by the devil.

SATANIC WORKS

In my own opinion, I think believers are too soft on the forces that are destroying humanity. The Bible says, "Jesus came to destroy the works of the devil." Destruction is not a joke. It says, "For this purpose, the Son of God was manifested that He might destroy the works of the devil" (I John 3:8). Jesus came to destroy the works of the destroyer. He came to crush the head of the serpent. You will agree with me that crushing the head of the serpent is not a gentle job.

Why do you think the apostles were so successful? They rough-handled the enemy. They manhandled demons, humiliated them and made them to cry like dogs.

There are many instances in the Acts of the Apostles where unclean spirits screamed and went out of many people. The apostles made evil spirits to beg for mercy by revealing their secrets. They made the enemies to depart in a hurry. By the time they finished with the evil spirits, nobody wanted to worship them again.

AN UNFRIENDLY RECEPTION

Believers are meant to cause trouble for the devil. When you give an unfriendly reception to a visitor, he generally does not wish to stay. When you give an unfavourable reception to the enemy, he will not want to stay. But when they come and you make the place very comfortable, they will sit down and dine with you. When you give them a hot reception they move away fast. When you make them so uncomfortable, they won't like to stay.

We have to deal with what the Bible calls the horse and his rider. The Bible says the horse and his rider, God has thrown into the sea. Perhaps, at a certain time, you looked for a solution to one problem or the other. Then you went to a witch doctor or somebody who was demonic and he laid hands on you. Know for sure that certain things might have been transferred into your body, like evil spirits and other kinds of deposits. These are things you must command to go out.

DESPATCHED FOR EVIL

If for instance, during your wedding some people, who you know are not born again Christians, laid hands on you, you need to pray. Do you know that that could completely change the course of your life? Some girls are dispatched to spoil the lives of some men. They carry out their evil assignment by planting evil things in the lives of these men. Likewise, some men are dispatched to some women for evil purpose.

Perhaps you have attended a dead church and while you were there, you used to see visions and speak in tongues but now that you are born again, you are still speaking their tongues and seeing their vision. You need deliverance. Those things have to go.

THE HORSES AND THE RIDERS

Some women wear beads on their waist. If you have done so, you need to pray well because those things are used to control the waist of many people. Some also have invisible waistbands which they are ignorant of. So, they are under foreign control.

In many places too, when a child is born, they consult their oracle to find out his future. They invite witch doctors or demonic prophets to prophesy. If they did that for you, you have to cancel their prophecy.

You have to battle both the horses and the riders. This is why the Bible says, "Jehovah, the Man of war, the Lord is His name." God does not deal with the horse and leave the rider alone, because the rider will live to fight another day.

VEHICLES OF ATTACK

The horse is the vehicle of attack while the rider is the attacker. But one thing is certain, the evil horse and the evil rider will fall into the Red Sea at the appointed time. They may run for a long time, but one day, the Lord Almighty will say, "Okay, you have done your worst, I have given you a long rope and you refused to repent." What follows then is cutting down.

When the cup of iniquity is full, God begins to act. They may harass and oppress God's people, they may insult them or tell them all kinds of things. The best thing to do in this type of situation is to keep quiet. The Bible says, "You shall keep your peace and I will do the fighting." If you could do the fighting, you would not be where you are. Do you see anyone cheating a child of God today? Don't worry. When God will begin to fight, you will not be surprised.

Sometimes it may even appear as if God does not care about what happens to you. But one day He will arise and the enemies shall scatter.

WAITING TIME

For many people the problem is the period between the time they cry to God and when God arises. It is a trying period for many people. The time God decides to arise is best known to Him. He programmes His work according to His will. He has His own time. And when it is His hour, the power of darkness cannot hold Him back. Notice this also that the devil and the powers of darkness have their own hour. But the important thing is that God never comes late.

GOD'S HOUR

Whatever God wants you to become, you will become, whether the devil likes it or not. When it is God's hour, even stones and other things will move into action. They will listen to their Maker.

For example in Revelation 20:13 we read:

"And the sea gave up the dead which were in it, and death and hell delivered up the dead which were in them."

When it is time and God says, "Let go," even the seas have no choice but to release what is in their hand. The same thing is recorded in Isaiah 43:5:

"Fear not, for I am with thee, I will bring thy seed from the east and gather thee from the west. I will say to the north, Give up; and to the south, Keep not back; bring my sons from far, and my daughters from the ends of the earth." Isaiah 43:5.

They have no option but to listen to their Maker.

THE GOSPEL OF PEACE

There are men who have collected spiritual power and want to help people. This is why the Bible says, "How beautiful are the feet of those that preach the gospel of peace?" That means that if the people preaching the gospel of peace enter into an environment, good luck and miracles will enter there and there shall be much joy in the place likewise.

CHAPTER FOUR
VICTORY OVER SATANIC MESSENGERS

The devil has his own vessels which he uses. He gives them dangerous weapon which they use against people. Sometimes he sends them to churches to cause confusion, or to homes to break them or to shops to spoil people's businesses. Sometimes, they introduce terrible problems.

It is a pity that some people allow themselves to be used by the devil. Anybody who submits himself or herself to be used by witchcraft spirit or familiar spirit, the Bible says, it shall be ill with him or her.

THE SATANIC VESSEL

After looking for a child for a long time, a couple in Uganda went to a witchdoctor who gave them certain things to eat. The woman got pregnant but then something strange began to happen. As her tummy was protruding, the tummy of her husband was protruding too. At the time the woman was about to give birth, the man too fell into labour. Then as the woman was delivered of the child, her husband died.

The witchdoctor was a vessel. May be the enemies

of the couple had been looking for ways of destroying them and never saw one. So, they prayed that one day the couple would come to their camp and that was exactly what happened. I know cases of people whose enemies sat on their text books or businesses and they did not move the way they should. We find many such evil vessels in the streets.

This is why believers should not laugh or make fun of people. There are many people in the streets who dress haggardly to provoke laughter and once you laugh at them, they transfer their problems to you. Why should you laugh at them anyway?

EVIL VESSELS

We have a lot of people living under the bridge. They go without food, clothes, and bath for weeks, yet they are stronger than those who sleep in air conditioned rooms. There is something extraordinary energising them. There are thousands of such vessels in the market place. They pick up people's goodness. They can also destroy. We have thousands of evil vessels in cinema houses. They are present at all the night parties. Believers should not go to night parties and should not hire any musician to play. Many people have put themselves into trouble because they wanted to display their wealth.

The thing about this world is that most times, the wicked people are hidden. You don't know them at all. Those who make noise about charms do not have anything. Such wicked people come to ceremonies where you display your wealth and you will serve them alcohol, and the angel of God will be recording how you are wasting God's money, how you are using it to feed your enemies and when they start fighting you, you will begin to call God. The musician you invited will not be able to help you.

POSSESSED PEOPLE

Many of the so-called prophets, prophetesses and holy mothers are possessed people with snakes and witchcraft spirits in them. They may prophesy and put on your head what has already been planned in their witchcraft gatherings. You may say, "But they carry Bibles." They carry Bibles to confuse you. If they do not carry Bibles, you will run away. Supposing they carry the head of a goat and begin to prophesy, nobody will wait.

Where is it written in the Bible that unless you bathe with black soap or special kind of soap, your problems will not be solved? Does a person need a physical bath before his prayers can be answered? Why should prayers be classified as special and ordinary? There are many of such vessels around confusing people and complicating matters for them.

SATANIC MESSENGERS

One day, as I was passing by somewhere, I saw one of the devil's evil vessels. He had padlocks, horns, etc. He said the padlock was to lock people up. As for the horn, he said if you wanted to displace your boss, all you needed do was to buy one horn, talk to it and that boss would just walk into the bush and you would take over his position. He even said that if you wanted to know whether your wife was unfaithful there was one you could use. I was shocked and people gathered round him to listen to what he was saying.

He said if somebody's life was not destroyed another person's life would not be good. He was saying this in an open place and some people were pricing and buying those items. The people who bought those things would use them against people around them who do not know anything about them.

EVIL VISITATION

A lot of people have what we call evil visitation, which is never in vain. When you are praying at night and suddenly, your head begins to swell up, know that somebody you cannot see is in that room. It is an evil visitor. When you feel a paralysing shock all over your body while praying, or you are being choked on your bed, or you have a cold feeling running down your body, or sudden intense fear and your heart starts to beat, know that strangers have come in. If you have experienced this before, you need to pray seriously because such visits are never in vain. They may even go away but they have planted what they wanted.

But why should they be sending such evil spirits to God's children and they go back home without any harm? It is an insult. Why, for example, should they dispatch an agent of the devil to your place of work without your knowing about it? Beloved, we need to sit up.

DIFFERENT PRAYERS

Now that we know from the Scriptures that they can be tormented, sent to a place they do not like to go and can be made to tremble, we must be very aggressive in our prayers against them. If somebody says, "I bind you," fine. He has prayed. If another person says, "I paralyse you," he too has prayed. But the prayer is a little bit different. Another person may say "Be roasted," he too has prayed, but in a different way. Another person can say, "Be swallowed after the order of Korah, Dathan and Abiram." He has prayed too in a different way. Another person can say, "Okay, is it I that you have gathered together against? Begin to fight yourself." They may start to fight and you start to wonder how you did it.

A STRANGE EXPERIENCE

I remember a pastor friend of mine who had a strange experience. One day, as he was praying for somebody, three demons came out and one of them gave the person he was praying for a terrible slap and the person fell down and died. My friend got angry and said, "What an insult? I am praying in this place and you demons have the audacity to come out and slap the person I am praying with. Okay, let me first deal with one of you." He faced one and commanded the ground to open up and swallow it. When the ground opened up, that one entered and it closed back. The other demons started shaking and begging him.

If you rough-handle demonic agents, when next they are assigned to you, they will say, "We are not going because the last time we went there, it was terrible." But if they came and you gave them a good reception, they will always come back. If they come and find out that you are fighting with your neighbour, they will say, "Fine, this is what we want." Or if they come and find that you are fighting with your spouse, or that you are busy watching a horrible film on the television, or you are doing a vigil with a cup of coffee by your side: you pray a little bit and sip the drink a little bit, they will say, "Fine, that is how we want it." They will swing into action. Beloved, we must not take it easy with the devil. Now is the time to rough-handle the enemy.

PRAYER POINTS

1. Father Lord, destroy the time-table of the enemy for my life, in the name of Jesus.
2. Every assignment of the devil in my life, business or home, I terminate you, in the name of Jesus.
3. All the trees of non-achievement, whether physical or spiritual, be uprooted, in the name of

Jesus.

4. Every spiritual vehicle employed against me, I command you to crash, in the name of Jesus.

5. I recover every stolen blessing starting from this week, in the name of Jesus.

6. Every evil horse and evil rider militating against me, be thrown into the sea, in the name of Jesus.

7. You spirit of anger, in whatever form you may be operating, loose your hold upon my life, in Jesus' name.

8. If you have ever worn a waist band, or something was attached to your waist so that you would not die, or you just wore it as an ornamental, use your two hands to hold your waist as you pray this prayer: "Lord Jesus, whatever evil has been done to me by the waist beads or band I wore, destroy it by the power in Your name.

9. I release myself from every bondage operating around my waist, in the name of Jesus.

10. If you recognise that when you were born certain information were collected from the demonic world on your behalf, lay your hands on hands on your head as you pray this one: Lord, You are the one that answereth by fire, let every demonic prophecy on my life at birth be cancelled now, in the name of Jesus.

1. A-Z of Complete Deliverance
2. Be Prepared
3. Bewitchment must die
4. Biblical Principles of Dream Interpretation
5. Born Great, But Tied Down
6. Breaking Bad Habits
7. Breakthrough Prayers For Business Professionals
8. Brokenness
9. Bringing Down The Power of God
10. Can God?
11. Can God Trust You?
12. Command The Morning
13. Consecration Commitment & Loyalty
14. Contending For The Kingdom
15. Connecting to The God of Breakthroughs
16. Criminals In The House Of God
17. Dealing With Hidden Curses
18. Dealing With Local Satanic Technology
19. Dealing With Satanic Exchange
20. Dealing With The Evil Powers Of Your Father's House
21. Dealing With Tropical Demons
22. Dealing With Unprofitable Roots
23. Dealing With Witchcraft Barbers
24. Deliverance By Fire
25. Deliverance From Spirit Husband And Spirit Wife
26. Deliverance From The Limiting Powers
27. Deliverance of The Brain
28. Deliverance Of The Conscience

29. Deliverance Of The Head
30. Deliverance: God's Medicine Bottle
31. Destiny Clinic
32. Destroying Satanic Masks
33. Disgracing Soul Hunters
34. Divine Military Training
35. Divine Yellow Card
36. Dominion Prosperity
37. Drawers Of Power From The Heavenlies
38. Evil Appetite
39. Evil Umbrella
40. Facing Both Ways
41. Failure In The School Of Prayer
42. Fire For Life's Journey
43. For We Wrestle ...
44. Freedom Indeed
45. Holiness Unto The Lord
46. Holy Cry
47. Holy Fever
48. Hour Of Decision
49. How To Obtain Personal Deliverance
50. How To Pray When Surrounded By The Enemies
51. Idols Of The Heart
52. Is This What They Died For?
53. Let God Answer By Fire
54. Limiting God
55. Madness Of The Heart
56. Making Your Way Through The Traffic Jam of Life

57. Meat For Champions
58. Medicine For Winners
59. My Burden For The Church
60. Open Heavens Through Holy Disturbance
61. Overpowering Witchcraft
62. Paralysing The Riders And The Horse
63. Personal Spiritual Check-Up
64. Power Against Coffin Spirits
65. Power Against Destiny Quenchers
66. Power Against Dream Criminals
67. Power Against Local Wickedness
68. Power Against Marine Spirits
69. Power Against Spiritual Terrorists
70. Power Must Change Hands
71. Pray Your Way To Breakthroughs
72. Prayer Is The Battle
73. Prayer Rain
74. Prayer Strategies For Spinsters And Bachelors
75. Prayer To Kill Enchantment
76. Prayer To Make You Fulfil Your Divine Destiny
77. Prayer Warfare Against 70 Mad Spirits
78. Prayers For Open Heavens
79. Prayers To Arrest Satanic Frustration
80. Prayers To Destroy Diseases And Infirmities
81. Prayers To Move From Minimum To Maximum
82. Praying Against The Spirit Of The Valley
83. Praying To Destroy Satanic Roadblocks
84. Praying To Dismantle Witchcraft

85. Principles Of Prayer
86. Release From Destructive Covenants
87. Revoking Evil Decrees
88. Safeguarding Your Home
89. Satanic Diversion Of The Black Race
90. Silencing The Birds Of Darkness
91. Slaves Who Love Their Chains
92. Smite The Enemy And He Will Flee
93. Speaking Destruction Unto The Dark Rivers
94. Spiritual Education
95. Spiritual Growth And Maturity
96. Spiritual Warfare And The Home
97. Strategic Praying
98. Strategy Of Warfare Praying
99. Stop Them Before They Stop You
100. Students In The School Of Fear
101. Symptoms Of Witchcraft Attack
102. The Baptism of Fire
103. The Battle Against The Spirit Of Impossibility
104. The Dinning Table Of Darkness
105. The Enemy Has Done This
106. The Evil Cry Of Your Family Idol
107. The Fire Of Revival
108. The Great Deliverance
109. The Internal Stumbling Block
110. The Lord Is A Man Of War
111. The Mystery Of Mobile Curses
112. The Mystery Of The Mobile Temple

113. The Prayer Eagle
114. The Power of Aggressive Prayer Warriors
115. The Pursuit Of Success
116. The Seasons Of Life
117. The Secrets Of Greatness
118. The Serpentine Enemies
119. The Skeleton In Your Grandfather's Cupboard
120. The Slow Learners
121. The Snake In The Power House
122. The Spirit Of The Crab
123. The star hunters
124. The Star In Your Sky
125. The Terrible Agenda
126. The Tongue Trap
127. The Unconquerable Power
128. The Unlimited God
129. The Vagabond Spirit
130. The Way Of Divine Encounter
131. The Wealth Transfer Agenda
132. Tied Down In The Spirits
133. Too Hot To Handle
134. Turnaround Breakthrough
135. Unprofitable Foundations
136. Vacancy For Mad Prophets
137. Victory Over Satanic Dreams
138. Victory Over Your Greatest Enemies
139. Violent Prayers Against Stubborn Situations
140. War At The Edge Of Breakthroughs

141. Wasting The Wasters
142. Wealth Must Change Hands
143. What You Must Know About The House Fellowship
144. When God Is Silent
145. When the Battle is from Home
146. When The Deliverer Need Deliverance
147. When Things Get Hard
148. When You Are Knocked Down
149. Where Is Your Faith
150. While Men Slept
151. Woman! Thou Art Loosed.
152. Your Battle And Your Strategy
153. Your Foundation And Destiny
154. Your Mouth And Your Deliverance

YORUBA PUBLICATIONS
1. ADURA AGBAYORI
2. ADURA TI NSI OKE NIDI
3. OJO ADURA

FRENCH PUBLICATIONS
1. PLUIE DE PRIERE
2. ESPIRIT DE VAGABONDAGE
3. EN FINIR AVEC LES FORCES MALEFIQUES DE LA MAISON DE TON PERE
4. QUE I'ENVOUTEMENT PERISSE
5. FRAPPEZ I'ADVERSAIRE ET IL FUIRA
6. COMMENT RECEVIOR LA DELIVRANCE DU MARI ET

30. NE GRAND MAIS LIE
31. POUVOIR CONTRE LES DEMOND TROPICAUX
32. LE PROGRAMME DE TRANFERT DE RICHESSE
33. LES ETUDIANTS A l'ECOLE DE LA PEUR
34. L'ETOILE DANS VOTRE CIEL
35. LES SAISONS DE LA VIE
36. FEMME TU ES LIBEREE

ANNUAL 70 DAYS PRAYER AND FASTING PUBLICATIONS

1. Prayers That Bring Miracles
2. Let God Answer By Fire
3. Prayers To Mount With Wings As Eagles
4. Prayers That Bring Explosive Increase
5. Prayers For Open Heavens
6. Prayers To Make You Fulfil Your Divine Destiny
7. Prayers That Make God To Answer And Fight By Fire
8. Prayers That Bring Unchallengeable Victory And Breakthrough Rainfall Bombardments
9. Prayers That Bring Dominion Prosperity And Uncommon Success
10. Prayers That Bring Power And Overflowing Progress
11. Prayers That Bring Laughter And Enlargement Breakthroughs
12. Prayers That Bring Uncommon Favour And Breakthroughs
13. Prayers That Bring Unprecedented Greatness & Unmatchable Increase
14. Prayers That Bring Awesome Testimonies And Turn Around Breakthroughs

FEMME DE NUIT
7. CPMMENT SE DELIVRER SOI-MEME
8. POVOIR CONTRE LES TERRORITES SPIRITUEL
9. PRIERE DE PERCEES POUR LES HOMMES D'AFFAIRES
10. PRIER JUSQU'A REMPORTER LA VICTOIRE
11. PRIERES VIOLENTES POUR HUMILIER LES PROBLEMES OPINIATRES
12. PRIERE POUR DETRUIRE LES MALADIES ET INFIRMITES
13. LE COMBAT SPIRITUEL ET LE FOYER
14. BILAN SPIRITUEL PERSONNEL
15. VICTOIRES SUR LES REVES SATANIQUES
16. PRIERES DE COMAT CONTRE 70 ESPIRITS DECHANINES
17. LA DEVIATION SATANIQUE DE LA RACE NOIRE
18. TON COMBAT ET TA STRATEGIE
19. VOTRE FONDEMENT ET VOTRE DESTIN
20. REVOQUER LES DECRETS MALEFIQUES
21. CANTIQUE DES CONTIQUES
22. LE MAUVAIS CRI DES IDOLES
23. QUAND LES CHOSES DEVIENNENT DIFFICILES
24. LES STRATEGIES DE PRIERES POUR LES CELIBATAIRES
25. SE LIBERER DES ALLIANCES MALEFIQUES
26. DEMANTELER LA SORCELLERIE
27. LA DELIVERANCE: LE FLACON DE MEDICAMENT DIEU
28. LA DELIVERANCE DE LA TETE
29. COMMANDER LE MATIN

www.ingramcontent.com/pod-product-compliance
Lightning Source LLC
Chambersburg PA
CBHW061300040426
42444CB00010B/2445